SELECTED POEMS

BY DAVID IGNATOW

Poems (1948)
The Gentle Weight Lifter (1955)
Say Pardon (1961)
Figures of the Human (1964)
Rescue the Dead (1968)
Poems 1934–1969 (1970)
The Notebooks of David Ignatow (1974)
Facing the Tree (1975)

DAVID
IGNATOW

Selected Poems

*Chosen, with Introductory Notes
and an Afterword, by*

ROBERT BLY

Wesleyan University Press

MIDDLETOWN, CONNECTICUT

Library of Congress Cataloging in Publication Data

Ignatow, David, 1914–
    David Ignatow : selected poems.

PS3517.G53A6   1975   811'.5'4   74–21924
ISBN 0–8195–4082–X
ISBN 0–8195–6039–1 pbk.

Manufactured in the United States of America
First edition

For Bill Bueno
with affection, admiration
and fondest memories

I feel along the edges of life
for a way
that will lead to open land.

Contents

I

Images of the Wild, Third Thing

Somewhere in all poetry that is alive, there are images of the knots of energy in the psyche that cannot be crushed, the energy that urges the baboon to leap suddenly on the jaguar, even knowing it will be killed, that urges the ship captain to come closer to shore, that encourages the painter to leave his wife and children and go to some Pacific island, that tells the saint not yet a saint it will be all right for him to spend the rest of his life in a cave, that makes the cockroach decide to become a butterfly, that appears as the dreamer falling is about to hit the earth, and slips him sideways and flows away with him out over the sea, and turns the sword into a transparent substance that can hurt no one, and allows a single hair to stir the sea. Psychologists notice that often the rational mind in anxiety can only think of two alternatives, usually involving opposites, and thereby thinks the situation deadlocked. Strangely, often a third thing the rational mind missed entirely enters, and solves it.

My beard rough as the beginning
of things, I'm new today.
You won't find me,
I'll be in the woods
growing a skin
to make friends
with the squirrels, the fox
and the puma; you won't catch me,
I'll be hidden behind their furry selves
and making my own sounds.
Look for me in the trees
or on the mountains,
if you can get away.

Mystique

No man has seen the third hand
that stems from the center,
near the heart. Let either
the right or the left prepare
a dish for the mouth,
or a thing to give,
and the third hand deftly
and unseen will change the object
of our hunger or of our giving.

Poem

A view of the mountain from the valley floor,
he who sees it understands,
and he who must read of it brings himself.
I cannot put him into words,
though his eyes move my thoughts to live.
I write of him
so that he may know my mountain.

The Gentle Weight Lifter

Every man to his kind of welcome in the world,
some by lifting cement barrels, laboring.
He looks so stupid doing it, we say.
Why not a soft job, pushing a pencil
or racketeering, the numbers game?
As the pattern is rigged, he must
get love and honor by lifting barrels.

It would be good to see a change,
but after barrels he cannot fool with intangibles.
He could with his muscular arm sweep them aside
and snarl the tiny lines
by which he can distinguish love.

He is fixed in his form,
save a hand reach from outside
to pick him up bodily and place him,
still making the movements that insure his love,
amidst wonders not yet arrived.

Brief Elegy

In every beautiful song is a promise of sleep.
I will sleep if you will sing to me,
but sing to me of sleep
when the bells have hushed in the towers
and the towers have hushed from their sounds.
Sing to me, strolling through silent streets.

To an Apple

You were rotten
and I sliced you into pieces
looking for a wholesome part,
then threw you into the street.
You were eaten by a horse,
dipping his head to nibble
gently at the skin.
I heard later he became violently ill,
died and was shipped off
to be processed. I think about it
and write of the good in you.

Two Voices

I'll challenge myself, I said.
I have read the classics;
my insides feel they'd like to be outside
catching air. It was cold
but sunny. I wore my coat,
no hat though. Adventure.
I would invite trouble at once.
Pneumonia. I'll escape Stendhal,
Baudelaire, Whitman, Eliot,
each pressing me in turn
to his heart. In the cold air
I hardened. Nearby stood a lake;
I jumped in.
         "We had to haul him
out, a block of ice, eyeballs
in a frozen stare. After melting him
down, we lost him. He had forgotten
how to breathe. 'Challenge the weather,'
he murmured. 'Challenge the weather.'
And he closed his eyes."

Doctor

The patient cries, Give me back feeling.
And the doctor studies the books:
what injection is suitable for hysterics,
syndrome for insecurity, hallucination?
The patient cries, I have been disinherited.
The doctor studies the latest bulletins
of the Psychiatric Institute and advises
one warm bath given at the moment of panic.
Afterwards inject a barbiturate. At this
the patient rises up from bed and slugs
the doctor and puts him unconscious to bed;
and himself reads the book through the night
avidly without pause.

Earth Hard

Earth hard to my heels
bear me up like a child
standing on its mother's belly.
I am a surprised guest to the air.

Say Pardon

Say pardon to a bum,
brushing past him.
He could lean back
and spit
and you would have to wipe it off.
How would you explain
that you have insulted
this man's identity,
of his own choosing;
and others could only scratch
their heads and advise you
to move on
and be quiet.
Say pardon
and follow your own will
in the open spaces ahead.

The Song

The song is to emptiness.
One may come and go
without a ripple. You see it
among fish in the sea,
in the woods among the silent
running animals, in a plane
overhead, gone; man
bowling or collecting coins,
writing about it.

A Loose Gown

I wear my life loosely around me,
feeling it at elbows and knees.
Sometimes I'm forced to hurry
and it races along with me,
taking the wind in its hollows.
I get out of breath
and would fall down exhausted
but the wind in these pockets
of my life keep me from falling.

The Bagel

I stopped to pick up the bagel
rolling away in the wind,
annoyed with myself
for having dropped it
as it were a portent.
Faster and faster it rolled,
with me running after it
bent low, gritting my teeth,
and I found myself doubled over
and rolling down the street
head over heels, one complete somersault
after another like a bagel
and strangely happy with myself.

East Bronx

In the street two children sharpen
knives against the curb.
Parents leaning out the window
above gaze and think and smoke
and duck back into the house
to sit on the toilet seat
with locked door to read
of the happiness of two tortoises
on an island in the Pacific—
always alone and always
the sun shining.

II

Working for a Living

The Paper Cutter

He slides the cut paper out
from under the raised knife.
His face does not lose interest.
"And now I go to my night job,"
he says cheerfully at five,
wiping his hands upon a rag.
He has stood all day in one spot,
pressing first the left
and then the right button.
"And what are you going to do
with all that money?" I ask.
His shoulders stick out bony.
"I will buy a house
and then I will lie down in it
and not get up all day," he laughs.

I See a Truck

I see a truck mowing down a parade,
people getting up after to follow,
dragging a leg. On a corner
a cop stands idly swinging his club,
the sidewalks jammed with mothers
and baby carriages. No one screams
or speaks. From the tail end
of the truck a priest and a rabbi intone
their prayers, a jazz band bringing up
the rear, surrounded by dancers and lovers.
A bell rings and a paymaster drives through,
his wagon filled with pay envelopes
he hands out, even to those lying dead
or fornicating on the ground.
It is a holiday called
"Working for a Living."

For One Moment

You take the dollar
and hand it to the fellow beside you
who turns and gives it to the next one
down the line. The world being round,
you stand waiting, smoking and lifting
a cup of coffee to your lips, talking
of seasonal weather and hinting
at problems. The dollar returns,
the coffee spills to the ground
in your hurry. You have the money
in one hand, a cup in the other,
a cigarette in your mouth,
and for one moment have forgotten
what it is you have to do,
your hair grey, your legs weakened
from long standing.

Love Poem for the Forty-Second Street Library

With my eyes turned to the sky
and my toes nearly touching pavement,
floating along I'll approach Times Square,
the cabs coming to a screeching halt,
whistles blowing and crowds on four corners
huddled together and staring,
my legs trailing above the ground,
my eyes lifted entranced
to the top of the Empire State Building
as they stare unbelievingly,
attaché cases and handbags weighing
them down, their backs aching.
I'll turn my shimmering gaze towards the Library,
my love for it spreading to the crowds
which will begin to sway softly and sing
to themselves of better days that have passed
and been forgotten. Children once with eyes
for everything, now their eyes on the dollar
which too hovers in front of them.

I'll glide up Fifth Avenue, my eyes focused
longingly on Central Park, on perhaps one small corner
where I will lie down and meditate,
and no crowds but each of us
spread in his favorite spot of lawn
or nearby shrub. I'll be followed
like the Holy Grail and later
go to jail for stopping traffic.
I'll turn my eyes upwards to the ceiling.
The warden and his wards will look
upwards with me in curiosity.

Oh judge, I'll plead, my toes trailing
the courtroom floor, I've been happy
this way, my eyes shimmering and turned
upwards to all things.

The Errand Boy I

To get quicker through the day
and to bring on night as a blessing,
to lie down in a sleep that is a dream
of completion, he takes up his package
from the floor—he has been ordered
to do so, heavy as it is, his knees weakening
as he walks, one would never know
by his long stride—and carries it
to the other end of the room.

I Want

I'll tell him I want to be paid immediately.
I'll sue him, I'll tear down his place,
I'll throw a fit, I'll show him whether
he can make me miserable.
I want things perfect.
I want to know I can expect a check
tomorrow morning at nine o'clock
exactly, with the mailman,
and if he doesn't bring it
I'll know that he too has done it
on purpose. He too knows
I have a family and a business
that are going to be made miserable by me.
At home I'll snarl and in the office
nobody will talk to me,
I'll talk to nobody,
and over the phone I'll whine
about money. Is that nice?
And what will people think of me?
It'll be some world,
a horrible one already,
the way I'm upset and with nothing to do
but rave, rave, rave.
I want my check!

Lunchtime

None said anything startling from the rest;
each held her coffee cup in her own way,
and one twanged, another whined and a third
shot out her phrases like a rear exhaust;
yet each stood for the same things:
the clothes in their conversation,
the food they ate and the men they could not
catch up with. They were not saying more
than could be said in a crowd, they made this
their unity, as the thinking of one person;
and getting up to go, lunch over
by the clock, each pulled out her own chair
from underneath her.

Notes for a Lecture

I will teach you to become American, my students:
take a turn at being enigmatic, to yourselves especially.
You work at a job and write poetry at night.
You write about working. Married,
you write about love.

I speak of kisses and mean quarrels,
the kiss brings the quarrel to mind,
of differences for their own sakes.

Did I ever think, going to bed,
a woman beside me would be no more uplifting
than a five-dollar raise? Since then
I've been uplifted in bed a hundred times
and but once raised in pay,
and that once has not been forgotten.

Take a broken whiskey bottle,
set it on top of your head
and dance. You have a costume,
you have meaning.

The Fisherwoman

She took from her basket four fishes
and carved each into four slices
and scaled them with her long knife,
this fisherwoman, and wrapped them;
and took four more and worked
in this rhythm through the day,
each action ending on a package
of old newspapers; and when it came
to close, dark coming upon the streets,
she had done one thing, she felt, well,
making one complete day.

Paymaster

The pay could have been more.
I felt I was giving myself
into his hands for judgment.
Thank you, he said, taking his check.
Thank me for what, I replied
silently. I am sending you home,
belittled in your own eyes.

The Dream

Someone approaches to say his life is ruined
and to fall down at your feet
and pound his head upon the sidewalk.
Blood spreads in a puddle.
And you, in a weak voice, plead
with those nearby for help;
your life takes on his desperation.
He keeps pounding his head.
It is you who are fated;
and you fall down beside him.
It is then you are awakened,
the body gone, the blood washed from the ground,
the stores lit up with their goods.

An Ecology

We drop in the evening like dew
upon the ground and the living
feel it on their faces. Death
soft, moist everywhere upon us,
soon to cover the living
as they drop. This explains
the ocean and the sun.

I stood in the center of a ring of faces.
Beyond them I could see a field of trees.
I moved and the faces moved with me,
I stopped and the faces stopped,
I dropped to the ground
and the ring lowered to my level.
One face opened its lips
and said, We are your fields.

III

What Clings like the Odor of a Goat

We know that behind every civilized person a primitive man is standing with his arms out, about to embrace the civilized person. The character of this primitive or instinctive man changes according to the intensities insisted on by the civilized man. If he has been forced to be adult too soon, his instinctive man will be infantile and pleasure-obsessed; if he or she insists on his or her friendliness, the instinctive man or woman will be cold and hostile; if the adult insists he is organized and rational, the primitive man will be obstructive, chaotic, and civilization-destroying. The primitive man may change the direction of his pressures and thrusts, even within the lifetime of the man, but he always clings as close as a shadow, in David Ignatow's phrase, his smell clings "tenaciously through perfume and a bath."

Ignatow in his Whitman poem notices the curious relationship between Whitman, one of his masters—the other two I guess to be Williams and Hemingway—and this primitive man. If the psyche insists that we shall all be friends, that we are friends, immediately cemeteries must be laid out for all those who will die soon of murder, rape, and insanity.

Communion

Let us be friends, said Walt,
and buildings sprang up
quick as corn and people
were born into them, stock
brokers, admen, lawyers and doctors
and they contended
                            among themselves
that they might know
                            each other.
Let us be friends, said Walt.
We are one and occasionally two
of which the one is made
and cemeteries were laid out
miles in all directions
to fill the plots with the old
and young, dead of murder, disease,
rape, hatred, heartbreak and insanity
to make way for the new
and the cemeteries spread over the land
their white scab monuments.

Let us be friends, said Walt, and the graves
were opened and coffins laid on top
of one another for lack of space.
It was then the gravediggers slit
their throats, being alone in the world,
not a friend to bury.

News Report

At two A. M. a thing, jumping out of a manhole,
the cover flying, raced down the street,
emitting wild shrieks of merriment and lust.
Women on their way from work, chorus girls
or actresses, were accosted with huge leers
and made to run; all either brought down
from behind by its flying weight, whereat
it attacked blindly, or leaping ahead,
made them stop and lie down.

Each, hysterical, had described it in her way,
one giving the shaggy fur, the next the shank bone
of a beast, and a third its nature
from which, as it seemed, pus dribbled,
when she saw no more—
                        all taking place
unnoticed until the first report, hours later
when consciousness was regained, and each
from diverse parts of the city has a telltale
sign, the red teeth marks sunk into the thigh
and the smell of a goat clinging tenaciously
through perfume and a bath.

And That Night

A photo is taken of the family
enjoying the sunshine
and that night someone sneaks up
from behind in your flat
as you sit reading the papers
and clobbers you. You never
find out why or who, you just
lean back and die.
The sunshine is gone too,
the photograph gets into the news.
You bring up a family in three small rooms,
this crazy man comes along
to finish it off.

No Theory

No theory will stand up to a chicken's guts
being cleaned out, a hand rammed up
to pull out the wriggling entrails,
the green bile and the bloody liver;
no theory that does not grow sick
at the odor escaping.

Sunday at the State Hospital

I am sitting across the table
eating my visit sandwich.
The one I brought him stays suspended
near his mouth; his eyes focus
on the table and seem to think,
his shoulders hunched forward.
I chew methodically,
pretending to take him
as a matter of course.
The sandwich tastes mad
and I keep chewing.
My past is sitting in front of me
filled with itself
and trying with almost no success
to bring the present to its mouth.

Blessing Myself

I believe in stillness,
I close a door
and surrender myself
to a wall and converse
with it and ask it
to bless me.
The wall is silent.
I speak for it,
blessing myself.

My son, my only death,
I give you your money
for the week. I leave,
happy and unhappy,
lightheaded, bewildered
at myself. Am I betrayed?
Where am I going without him?

I am alone here among trees and fields.
We were together and I loved your pauses
and difficulty in speaking.
I was warmed by your problem,
a man who would speak calmly,
making decision. I was all for that.

You came from behind doors
unlocked for you, remained silent
until I grew silent
and then you spoke
of the one in you
hidden away
to whom you owe much
and who will come for that reason
and demand you entirely.

It is peace coming to claim you,
your face laboring and grave.

A Political Cartoon

Ten men are seated around a conference table, each with a sign attached to the back of the head giving his title. However, each stands up in turn to identify himself. "I am the Secretary of the Interior." "I am the Secretary of the Treasury." "I am the Secretary of Agriculture." I am the Secretary of Housing and Urban Development." "Secretary of Commerce." "Health, Education and Welfare." And so on. Finally, a slow, deliberative figure rises to his feet and announces solemnly that he is the President.

He sits down with dignity. A gun is lying in front of him on the table. He shakes his head at it sorrowfully and pushes it gently across the table to the Secretary of the Interior, who cocks the gun and pushes it carefully to the Secretary of Commerce seated beside him. The Secretary of Commerce fondles it and puts it to his ear as if listening for a sound of life and then shoves it across the table to the Attorney General, who takes it and holds it up to his eyes admiringly, turning it over and over in his hands. He thrusts it at the Secretary of State, who pulls back alarmed but then manages to take it in his nervous hands. He has made the others smile and laugh softly. A joking undercurrent makes itself felt. He bravely twirls the gun around his finger, striking a nonchalant pose, one arm draped across the back of his chair. The gun whirls off his finger and is caught with both hands with a shout of fright by the Secretary of Health, Education and Welfare at whom the gun has been flying. As he catches it with almost a comical motion laughter explodes around the table, joined in by the President who however is shaking his head in disapproval.

Now the gun is being passed rapidly from hand to hand as in a game of bean bag. It suddenly fires, sending everyone diving beneath the table except the Secretary of the Interior. He is slumped across the table, blood spreading over its surface. Some time passes before the others come up from beneath the table and reseat themselves. They stare at the dead man. The President, sitting erect and firmly in his chair, has resumed the dignity of his office. Again the gun lies in front of him and he plays with it idly, musing, sad and grim. He shakes his head, holds the gun up to his eyes and examines it with distaste, then stands up slowly, a hand upon his chest. He begins silently to mouth his words in a speech addressed to the Cabinet, his free hand pointing tragically at the weapon lying on the table in front of him. Following a long peroration with appropriate gestures, he turns his attention to the gun, talking directly at it in accusatory style, climaxed by an imperious gesture of his thumb for the weapon to leave the room. He then sits down in exhaustion and mops his brow. With anger and disgust he pushes the gun across the table to the Attorney General, who slides it gently towards the Secretary of Agriculture. It goes the round of the table and just as it is about to be returned to the President it goes off again. The Secretary of Commerce falls back against his chair, his head drops loosely onto his shoulder. He is dead. All the others bow their heads and clasp their hands on the table in front of them in sorrowful prayer.

The silence suddenly is shattered by the blare of a truck horn outside behind the conference room door. The double doors roll up like garage doors to show a real truck standing behind them, its motor racing and backfiring. The truck rolls in and circles the room, its chassis heaped with grain. The truck stops and backs up against the table between the President and the Secretary of Agriculture and begins to unload, tipping the chassis upwards. The grain slides down, burying beneath it the table, up to the waist of everyone seated around it. The President, in the meanwhile, has dug the gun out of the grain from in front of the body of the Secretary of Commerce and hands it without comment to the Secretary of Health, Education and Welfare, who accepts it with a grave nod and gives it to the Secretary of State. It starts to make the rounds of the table again. It is also offered to the two dead gentlemen as a token of lasting respect. In the meantime, the truck has left empty while another has backed into the room with still another load. It too is deposited upon the conference table and the cabinet members are buried beneath it over their heads, except for the President who has received the gun and is standing and firing deliberately and with dignity, until he too is buried above his head, including his upraised hand gripping the gun. All the while it is I who have been driving the truck into the conference room and spilling the grain.

How Come?

I'm in New York covered by a layer of soap foam.
The air is dense from the top of skyscrapers
to the sidewalk in every street, avenue
and alley, as far as Babylon on the East,
Dobbs Ferry on the North, Coney Island
on the South and stretching far over
the Atlantic Ocean. I wade
through, breathing by pushing
foam aside. The going is slow,
with just a clearing ahead
by swinging my arms. Others are groping
from all sides, too. We keep moving.
Everything else has happened here
and we've survived: snow storms,
traffic tieups, train breakdowns, bursting
water mains; and now I am writing
with a lump of charcoal stuck between my toes,
switching it from one foot to the other—
this monkey trick learned visiting
with my children at the zoo of a Sunday.
But soap foam filling the air,
the bitter, fatty smell of it . . . How come?
My portable says it extends to San Francisco!
Listen to this, and down to the Mexican border
and as far north as Canada. All the prairies,
the Rocky Mountains, the Great Lakes, Chicago,
the Pacific Coast. No advertising stunt
could do this. The soap has welled out of the ground,
says the portable suddenly. The scientists report
the soil saturated. And now what?
We'll have to start climbing for air,
a crowd forming around the Empire State Building
says the portable. God help the many
who will die of soap foam.

Against the Evidence

As I reach to close each book
lying open on my desk, it leaps up
to snap at my fingers. My legs
won't hold me, I must sit down.
My fingers pain me
where the thick leaves snapped together
at my touch.
          All my life
I've held books in my hands
like children, carefully turning
their pages and straightening out
their creases. I use books
almost apologetically. I believe
I often think their thoughts for them.
Reading, I never know where theirs leave off
and mine begin. I am so much alone
in the world, I can observe the stars
or study the breeze, I can count the steps
on a stair on the way up or down,
and I can look at another human being
and get a smile, knowing
it is for the sake of politeness.
Nothing must be said of estrangement
among the human race and yet
nothing is said at all
because of that.
But no book will help either.
I stroke my desk,
its wood so smooth, so patient and still.
I set a typewriter on its surface
and begin to type
to tell myself my troubles.
Against the evidence, I live by choice.

Leaping from Ambush

A man goes by with a woman.
Another man cleaning his car
by the curb glances at her
and follows with his eyes
but returns to wiping his car
with a chamois cloth.
                    Is it
the chamois cloth that stops him
from killing the man and leaping
upon the woman?

Ritual One

As I enter the theatre the play is going on.
I hear the father say to the son on stage,
You've taken the motor apart.
The son replies, The roof is leaking.
The father retorts, The tire is flat.
Tiptoeing down the aisle, I find my seat,
edge my way in across a dozen kneecaps
as I tremble for my sanity.
I have heard doomed voices calling on god the
    electrode.
Sure enough, as I start to sit
a scream rises from beneath me.
It is one of the players.
If I come down, I'll break his neck,
caught between the seat and the backrest.
Now the audience and the players on stage,
their heads turned towards me, are waiting
for the sound of the break. Must I?
Those in my aisle nod slowly, reading my mind,
their eyes fixed on me, and I understand
that each has done the same.
Must I kill this man as the price of my admission
to this play? His screams continue loud and long.
I am at a loss as to what to do,
I panic, I freeze.

My training has been to eat the flesh of pig.
I might even have been able to slit a throat.
As a child I witnessed the dead chickens
over a barrel of sawdust absorbing their blood.
I then brought them in a bag to my father
who sold them across his counter. Liking him,
I learned to like people and enjoy their company
    too,
which of course brought me to this play.
But how angry I become.

Now everybody is shouting at me to sit down,
sit down or I'll be thrown out.
The father and son have stepped off stage
and come striding down the aisle side by side.
They reach me, grab me by the shoulder
and force me down. I scream, I scream,
as if to cover the sound of the neck breaking.

All through the play I scream
and am invited on stage to take a bow.
I lose my senses and kick the actors in the teeth.
There is more laughter
and the actors acknowledge my performance with a
    bow.
How should I understand this?
Is it to say that if I machine-gun the theatre
from left to right they will respond with applause
that would only gradually diminish with each death?
I wonder then whether logically I should kill myself
too out of admiration. A question indeed,
as I return to my seat and observe a new act
of children playfully aiming their kicks
at each other's groins.

Ritual Two

The kids yell and paint their bodies
black and brown, their eyes bulging.
As they brush, they dance, weaving
contorted shapes. They drive each other
to the wall, to the floor, to the bed,
to the john, yelling, "Nothing!"

Now they race around in a circle,
pounding their bellies, and laughter
rises from among them. They begin
to take the stage apart on which they stand,
ripping, kicking and pounding.
I show them my palm,
the cavity of my mouth down to my larynx
and then as I begin my own dance—
it ends when I die—they lock hands
and circle around me, very glad, very comforted
for the cirlce shall be empty of me
and they, falling through the stage, will yell,
"Nothing!"
            I remove hat, coat, shoes, socks, pants
and undershirt. I make motions to the ceiling
to come down and make motions to the floor to open.
I pretend to write a check for all my money
and hand it around. Each refuses to take it
and continues to dance. I give the check
to a hand that reaches from the ceiling,
as the kids chant, "Nothing, Nothing!"

I pretend to hold a child by the hand
and walk as though strolling up a street
with him and stoop to listen to this child
and talk to him, when suddenly I act
as if shot, slowly falling to the ground,
kissing the child goodby with my fingertips,
but I spring up and pretend to be the child,

lost, abandoned, bewildered, wanting to die,
crouching as the circle keeps chanting,
"Nothing, Nothing!"
I then rise slowly to my full height,
having grown up through my agony.
I throw my head back proudly
and join hands with others as they dance,
chanting their theme. We converge in the center,
bang against each other, scream and scatter.

Self-Employed
For Harvey Shapiro

I stand and listen, head bowed,
to my inner complaint.
Persons passing by think
I am searching for a lost coin.
You're fired, I yell inside
after an especially bad episode.
I'm letting you go without notice
or terminal pay. You just lost
another chance to make good.
But then I watch myself standing at the exit,
depressed and about to leave,
and wave myself back in wearily,
for who else could I get in my place
to do the job in dark, airless conditions?

Spring

The mountain in its blue haze
should be praised;
the lake too
at the foot of the mountain.
It stretches into the distance
like an invitation to die
into the air, elated.

Dilemma

Whatever we do, whether we light
strangers' cigarettes—it may turn out
to be a detective wanting to know who is free
with a light on a lonely street nights—
or whether we turn away and get a knife
planted between our shoulders for our discourtesy;
whatever we do—whether we marry for love
and wake up to find love is a task,
or whether for convenience to find love
must be won over, or we are desperate—
whatever we do; save by dying,
and there too we are caught,
by being planted too close to our parents.

Epitaph

There were no hidden motives to his life,
he is remembered for his meanness.
Beyond that we may look into the sky
and lose ourselves in the blue air.

And the Same Words

I like rust on a nail,
fog on a mountain.
Clouds hide stars,
rooms have doors,
eyes close,
and the same words
that began love
end it
with changed emphasis.

For My Mother Ill

I'll join you in your sleep,
into the same darkness dive,
where dead fish float together.
But we shall be communing,
blindly and without feeling;
but by knowing now,
as I lie back upon a pillow,
as you close your eyes,
the comfort of it.

Playfully

Lovely death of the horse
lying on its side, legs bent
as in gallop, and firm policeman
pointing his gun at the horse's head:
dull sound of the shot, twitch
along the body, the head
leaping up from the ground
and dropping—
to hold me by its death
among children
home from school, the sky calm.

Playfully, I note my grey head.

Last Night

Last night I spoke to a dead woman with green face.
She told me of her good life among the living,
with a faithful man. He was right there
beside her as tall as I, and moving
like me, with kind motions. If she did breathe,
it was just to talk and tell her life
in their basement smelling moist
like freshly opened earth. He was good to her
and she had worked as a typist
every day and came home to cook.
It was a good life with her husband,
he was kind; and she took hold of his hand
and said, "In this basement we've made a home,
with me working as typist and he studying
his music." She was dead, that much she understood
herself by her tone; and she looked at me
with green eyes.

Beautiful and Kind

Outside my window
floats the head of a woman
looking in. Strangely,
I live on the top floor.
She reminds me of the one
in my dream—serene,
beautiful and kind,
in whom all said shines
with goodness on her face,
even as I denounce her a fraud.
I must kiss her, I say in gratitude,
and prepare to step out the window.

Brief Cases

It was then that carrying brief cases
was prohibited in public as a mark
of impotence; no man need disgrace himself,
not recognizing his own shortcomings,
obvious to others, especially police
who carried their nightsticks
in their hands.

           "What are men if not men,"
was the motto they wore on their caps
in red and white, with scarves twirled
around their throats, of any color
for their pride. And the women,
oh the women, were unhappy.

It was then that carrying brief cases
in public was prohibited to them too,
for in these brief cases were tiny men
packed neatly in small cartons
to be opened in private homes.
Oh the little men danced on the tables
and kissed the lips of the women
who gave their lips to be kissed,
and the tall men who carried the brief cases
withdrew into the dark rooms of the houses.

Oh the women were not happy
but the tiny men grew tall
and all brief cases were abolished
and replaced by beds
that were then carried on the strong backs
of the tall men who once were little.
Oh the women were not happy,
nor the tall men with all the little habits
of the past

           How did it all end?
I'm hard put to tell you but I did hear

that the women chose to live
and the once little men and those
withdrawn into the dark
gave birth.

IV

The Struggle between the Statistical Mentality and Eros

"The faces that judge me," Ignatow asks, "are they all kindly?" He has the sense that if he looks impersonal, they will pick him up "like a stone," and use him for something. If he doesn't look and act impersonal, and if he has no money, they are the "life and death of his power." As we know, both American capitalism and Russian communism are shot through with disastrous conflicts built into the system between Eros consciousness and the statistical mentality. Both cultures fall into Vietnams and Gulag Archipelagos by being insensitive to the boundaries of feeling. A shoemaker in the Middle Ages—Jacob Boehme I think of—could be in business and yet never have to slide into statistical mentality, since he probably knew everyone who bought shoes from him, and one works on a shoe long enough so that love energy can rest in it, even for a few moments. But it's clear that business in quantity, that is most post-Industrial-Revolution business, requires that Eros consciousness be given up, and the love energy pulled back inside. A man suffers in the end as much as a woman if he is constantly being pushed sideways into statistical mentality, and away from the "road of feeling." Ignatow notices that the zoo is a good symbol for that slide to statistical mentality, since the animal still has his instinctive Eros, but the Eros consciousness has nothing to hold to. As Rilke said, a picture enters through the eyes of a zoo tiger, goes down to the heart, and there simply ceases existing.

Television news leads us to take in images of suffering, and then get used to seeing the images die the moment they hit the heart. Our feeling-impulse wants us to stop the TV program, and relieve the suffering, and since it cannot, the impulse fades and dies. We all become objective and businessmen. "The businessman is a traitor to himself first of all, and then no one else matters." If love energy cannot coexist with the statistical mentality, death energy can. A businessman said to Ignatow shortly before he died: "I have a big deal on, I want you in on it."

A First on TV
For Walter Cronkite

This is the twentieth century,
you are there, preparing to skin
a human being alive. Your part
will be to remain calm
and to participate with the flayer
in his work as you follow his hand,
the slow, delicate way with the knife
between the skin and flesh,
and see the red meat emerge.
Tiny rivulets of blood will flow
from the naked flesh and over the hands
of the flayer. Your eyes will waver
and turn away but turn back to witness
the unprecedented, the incredible,
for you are there
and your part will be to remain calm.

You will smash at the screen
with your fist and try to reach
this program on the phone, like a madman
gripping it by the neck
as it were the neck of the flayer
and you will scream into the receiver,
"Get me Station ZXY at once, at once,
do you hear!" But your part
will be to remain calm.

In Place of Love

In place of love we must have money:
fifteen thousand for her house
the woman requires, not a penny less—
standing fine-lipped in her parlor.
Grey-haired, though young in the hips
and eyes. A little smile, perhaps
a return motion of the hips,
would bring the price closer to love.

From male to male she looks
for whom to trust in the bargaining,
the son or the father—here to buy.
And the house empty, save for a sister
her own greying age, dishwashing
in the kitchen. A man's voice, laughing
but gentle, and the clatter stops;
a chalk face peeks past the door:
a little love. The parlor couch torn
in the middle shows no love.
She who is fine-lipped looks hastily
at the tear, and stammers about "no time,"
the house in disrepair. No doubt,
and the eyes blue and direct explain
what is missing.
                    With tea between her
and the guests, her own laughter warmed
from the tension of her lips, the price too
has begun to ease: a wavering
between thirteen and fourteen.
Her arm draped over the couch,
sat in gracefully, the hand begins to caress
the cloth absentmindedly.

Emergency Clinic

Come in with your stab wound up the middle.
You say two cars collided, you caught
in between—and your breath stinks
of liquor. You were found staggering
under the Atlantic Avenue El
in the empty street outside a bar;
a figure escaping into the dark—
someone known to you, no doubt,
with whom leaning over a drink
you discussed white men
with jocular hatred. Is there no
comradeship in misery either?
Less drunk than you, therefore more desperate,
it was his turn to use the knife,
as it was yours no doubt, some night before
on the case now in the morgue,
or if not you then someone who could stand
in your place and will lie in your place
tomorrow. Do not bother to tell me
the truth, since you do presume I know
by your graceless dodge. You know comradeship
in our shared knowledge,
in the anger that I feel towards you
and towards myself.

The White Ceiling

Until that child, one flight below, stops crying,
struck by its mother, I cannot sleep—
until it is hushed up by kindness,
a stroke silently, softly given upon its head.
Why not, I think, go downstairs in my bathrobe,
knock gently on the door and ask permission,
"If you don't mind," so that I too
may sleep.
           There was an argument
between parents about money; not altogether;
their voices personal as money is not.
In the hush of an unhappy truce the slap sounded.
Since those below are helpless, I lie here
and look up at the white ceiling.

With the Door Open

Something I want to communicate to you,
I keep my door open between us.
I am unable to say it,
I am happy only
with the door open between us.

Content

I should be content
to look at a mountain
for what it is
and not as a comment
on my life.

The businessman is a traitor to himself first
of all and then no one else matters,
hardened, sick of himself.

                              I once knew
someone like that and he died in a chair.
It was sad for the chair, sold
and nobody knows now who has it.
The funeral had ten Cadillacs
filled with friends. I was there.
I was last to talk to him
or rather he talked to me
and said, I've got a big deal on
and want you in on it.

The Business Life

When someone hangs up, having said
to you, "Don't come around again,"
and you have never heard the phone
banged down with such violence
nor the voice vibrate with such venom,
pick up your receiver gently and dial
again, get the same reply; and dial
again, until he threatens. You will
then get used to it, be sick only
instead of shocked. You will live,
and have a pattern to go by, familiar
to your ear, your senses and your dignity.

Nice Guy

I had a friend and he died. Me.
I forgot to mourn him that busy day
earning a living. I heard a click
telling me his eyes had closed
for the last time inside me,
and I turned away, not of my own volition,
but getting an offer of a job
I answered politely, saying yes,
his death unfortunate at midday
during business. I apologized
but had no one to apologize to,
buried without me at work.
I mourn him now at leisure on the couch
after the day. He was a good guy,
he meant well, only he had lost his teeth
and had to swallow whole.
He died of too much.

The faces that judge me,
are they all kindly?
The power they have,
is it all for good?
With no money of my own,
they are the life and death
of my power. My fright
warns me that to look
impersonal is to be taken up
like a stone.

A Guided Tour through the Zoo

Ladies and gentlemen,
these are pygmies, fated to live
in small perspective; children
of their shrunk parents, who
because of stubborn pride fed
on small seeds and herbs, scrabbled
together with hooded eyes; and so
were grown to such likeness; but
in turn had been shut in by their parents
in caves to be told night was day;
for their parents' parents were fledged
on the precipice from which they fled
to these caves, and so on, giving us
this tribe before us.
                    The story is sad,
for they remember by lost meanings
of words that they were of Hercules,
who could move earth for fleas to rest
easy, or sheep to roll softly downhill.
They were men, so called, in their unworded
language, which, when the sun grows brutal
with them as with rocks, they cry
remembrance in these open fields,
their homes under the short grass.
Ladies and gentlemen, let us move on
now to the cage of wild wolves.

The Debate

This man brings me stones
out of the ground. These
are eggs, he says, of the Jurassic
age, hardened. They may
be looked upon as eggs.
And taking them in awe
I drop them. They bounce,
one strikes me on the toe,
I wince. They are eggs,
he repeats calmly.
They are stone, I shout.
Stone, stone! They were eggs
in their day and bruise me now.
They are eggs, ossified,
he amends calmly.
And I will not let you
fry them for breakfast,
I answer sweetly,
because they are stone.

Nurse

The old man who can undress before you
as easily as before a mirror believes
that you are only the matured concept of his body,
as idea only.

Let us hope your uniform does not deceive him,
in that you are dedicated to his care.
The dress you wear is white for the abolition
of all your woes before his;
for he has worn the body of his time
a little longer and a little more indulgently
than you, whose cries of welcome or goodby
beneath his window on your night leave
will wake him fitfully from the dream
of the burden of earth given back to earth again.

You are to know that body is love
of having been born and to grow old
is to be born into returning to the good
from which he came.
You have eyes to see no shame
but resignation in his stooped figure,
such as love brings.

And now, your own eyes are colorless of wrong,
and every look is to follow
one man's devotion to being old.
You take his clothes from him,
and let him rest;
and in your going to and fro
from cabinet to cot carry instruments
of your respect to his side.

V

Living in the City

It's clear that in our society, the demonic is generally repressed. Very few people are in touch with a private source of wildness inside them, let alone so close to it or he or she that they can confidently give the source a name, as Socrates did, and as many Sufis, to mention a more recent group of "wild men," have done. What is meant by "mass-man" in fact seems to be a state in which for large groups of people the private source of wildness is inaccessible. They have to look sideways then, to those around them, for assurance as to who they are.

But if I am not my demonic wildness, then who am I? Nobody. The zoo lion

> gets up from the couch under the closed window
> and walks over to the rear wall
> where he lies down again upon a sofa
> as a change, as a protest.
> He has nothing to say, looks out at you,
> but then he might turn on his wife
> and tear her to pieces. It would
> extend the borders of his life
> and sex means nothing.
> For days he lies alongside the wall.

More and more often, we have another experience of nobody-ness. A man watching television gets to know the television "personalities," but they do not know him. The man in New York knows the Mayor, but the Mayor does not know him. David Ignatow describes the strange experience of speaking once, as an admitting clerk at a Brooklyn Hospital, to Zero Mostel, telling Zero Mostel that his mother had died. The poem describes the longing Ignatow had that Mostel should know him, as Ignatow "knew" him. You know the President of your corporation, but the President does not know you. The only conclusion the unconscious can draw then is that you don't exist. In that state, it is easy for the impersonal demonic to invade the isolated person, and pull him away from the community entirely through insanity:

> One out of insanity breaks loose:
> he could not make that extra effort
> to keep connected with us. Loneliness

> like a wheeling condor was attracted
> to the particle that had strayed apart.

Rollo May in his *Love and Will* describes well this pull toward possession by the impersonal—as opposed to personal—demonic, palpable now in great cities, where the impersonalization is growing. "The most severe punishment Yahweh could inflict on his people was to blot out their names. 'Their names,' Yahweh proclaims, 'shall be wiped out of the book of the living.'"

David Ignatow's range of feeling includes that terrible wiped-out-of-the-book-of-the-living feeling, the emptiness that invites possession, and so he knows very well that he is capable of the violence that most white poets reserve in their minds for "others." Doing violence is a way of proving that you can still affect others, and thereby do exist. David Ignatow has had to make a place in his work for violence that is not "personal." Can we say that Yeats did not have that problem?

By giving impersonal violence a place in his work, and yet not yielding to it, as the writers of television scripts do, the wheeling condors are refused his body.

The Zoo Lion

He gets up from the couch under the closed window
and walks over to the rear wall
where he lies down again upon a sofa
as a change, as a protest.
He has nothing to say, looks out at you,
but then he might turn on his wife
and tear her to pieces. It would
extend the borders of his life
and sex means nothing.
For days he lies alongside the wall.

Sales Talk

Better than to kill each other off
with our extra energy is to run after the bus,
though another be right behind. To run
and to explain to ourselves we have no time
to waste, when it is time that hangs
dangerously on our hands, so that the faster
we run the quicker the breezes rushing by
take time away.
          For comfort we must work
this way, because in the end we find
fume-filled streets and murder headlines:
one out of insanity breaks loose:
he could not make that extra effort
to keep connected with us. Loneliness
like a wheeling condor was attracted
to the particle that had strayed apart.
The brief case we carry, the pressed trousers,
the knotted tie under a white collar add up
to unity and morale.

Where Nothing is Hidden

Now I understand myself running back
to the city, out of breath and happy
to have escaped the sight of green vomit
and the groaning power lawn mower—
this advertised peace. I wanted
truly undisguised faces of boredom
swirling around me in the street
and my own grim hail to traffic jams,
to death by cops' cross fire,
to dope addiction,
to married life in Brooklyn overlooking the cemeteries
and to the crumbling beer-can-littered schoolyards
of Harlem.
Nothing is hidden.
Nobody lies or covers up.
A low gas cloud covers the city
on which the people slowly choke in bed
but not one's own green vomit to walk on
in silence. It hangs a curtain from the trees.

Scream and yell and pound on the walls here in
    the city,
to be ignored or beaten down.
Speak of the bitter with your last breath
and sweep the whole city into the sea
with a gesture or drive your car off the dock,
taking with you the city's death,
but none of the green vomit
of those who spill their guts
and stand on it in silence like trees
that hide their birds from one another
and live for hundreds of years
without comment.

Promenade

His head split in four parts,
he walks down the street—pleasant
with shady trees and a sun softened
by leaves touching it. He walks,
a revolving turret for a head,
from each slit of which he looks guardedly:
the enemy approaches or he approaches
the enemy. At any moment the chatter of differences
will break out; the four parts of his skull
revolve slowly, seeking the time.

In there they do not know of each other,
sealed off by steel walls. They are safer
together, singly and apart;
while overhead, ignored in the walk,
are the leaves, touching each other and the sun.

Pricing

The grave needed a stone marker.
We picked Flint Rock from New England,
four feet high and three feet wide,
to cover two bodies lying side by side,
my mother and eventually my father.
He stood examining it with us,
his son and two sons-in-law,
in the marble store, and made no comment
other than the weary, grim look
of an old man who has lost his wife,
his only companion, and himself soon to go,
alone now, living among strangers,
though they were his kin.
An old man shuts himself off.
Later after the purchase, as I drove the car,
he tried to say something
to convey his mood and failed,
saying something hackneyed, conscious of it,
and said nothing further, until at home
finally with his daughter he discussed
the price and the stone's color
and its width.

Moving Picture

When two take gas
by mutual consent
and the cops come in
when the walls are broken down
and the doctor pays respects
by closing the books
and the neighbors stand about
sniffing and afraid
and the papers run a brief
under a whiskey ad
and the news is read
eating ice cream or a fruit
and the paper is used
to wrap peelings
and the garbage man
dumps the barrel
into the truck
and the paper flares
in the furnace and sinks back
charred and is scooped up
for mud flats and pressed down
by steam rollers for hard ground
and a house on it
for two to enter.

Get the Gasworks

Get the gasworks in a poem
and you've got the smoke and smokestacks,
the mottled red and yellow tenements,
and grimy kids who curse with the pungency
of the odor of gas. You've got America, boy.

Sketch in the river, and barges,
all dirty and slimy.
How do the seagulls stay so white?
And always cawing like little mad geniuses?
You've got the kind of living
that makes the kind of thinking we do:
gaswork smokestack whistle tooting wisecracks.

They don't come because we like it that way,
but because we find it outside our window every
       morning,
in soot on the furniture,
and trucks carrying coal for gas,
the kid hot after the ball under the wheel.
He gets it over the belly, alright.
He lies there.

So the kids keep tossing the ball around
after the funeral.
So the cops keep chasing them,
so the mamas keep hollering,
and papa flings his newspaper outward,
in disgust with discipline.

An Illusion

She was saying mad things,
like To hell with the world!
Love is all you need! Go on
and get it! What are you
waiting for! And she walked,
more like shuffled up the street,
her eyes fixed in the distance.
She would not divert them
for a moment. People stepped
self-consciously out of the way.
Straight up stood her hair, wild.

What are you waiting for, snarled
from her lips; it seemed directed
really to herself, to someone inside
with whom she fought. The shredded hem
of her dress rustled around her.

Off to the Cemetery

To die is to be brought down among blacks
and Puerto Ricans who live in rat buildings
and inject themselves to endure
the wastes of newsprint in the street.
To die is to be abandoned to the Sanitation
Department that comes to remove you
quickly in an oblong garbage box,
the men ashamed of their uniforms.

The funeral is attended with studied
preparations for a wedding. The event
grows happy and relieved as it concludes
and the body is removed from the chapel.
Then all get to file out. The ceremony
was not to see the departed off
to an eternal rest, life transitory
if blessed, but for a pact, a vow
of renewed heat, life married to death
and made one, and away the guests go
to the cemetery in cars and cabs
that are as good-looking as false teeth.

Side by Side

What does it mean to be mature?
We have got to take hold of the fellow
we work with and whom we trust to be true
to us in a crisis and say to him,
gripping him by the shirt front
near the throat, our face thrust into his:
snarl at him, "Now look here, I see clear
through you, playing me for a sucker
by being nice to me. You want to get away
with something without paying for it.
I am not going to let you, see?
I am not going to be taken advantage of,
and when I get the chance to do what I want
I shall do it with much more ruthlessness
than you and not be tied up in feelings.
After that I shall be friends with you,
once I have what I want from you."
This being maturity, I turn to him
as we sit side by side working
and say aloud so that it may be heard
all over, "Give me a cigarette, will you,
I'm all out of them."

The Appointment Card

He flashes a knife and waves it under our noses
as he sways from seat to seat where passengers sit
quietly waiting for him to pass by. He curses us
and leers and makes menacing gestures of cutting up
into small pieces each and every one of us.
We watch, we wait. Soon, soon the train will reach
its stop and we'll get off. He strikes a face.
The person screams and collapses. The knifer
stands over him, looking down, waiting to decide,
waiting for his thought. Perhaps it is the person
on the floor who must act it out for him.
If he gets up, stab again. If he moans, stab again.
If he seeks to crawl away whimpering and begging
not to be touched again, strike anyhow.
The rest of us seated look on,
frozen by a sudden recognition of absurdity.
Is this the brutality and horror
which we feared until now and is not feared any longer,
so ordinary compared to what we feared? Let it pass.
Let this worst pass. It could be worse still.
Let us continue to live humiliated
and defeated because there is nothing to rebel against,
the cause mundane, a life, another life, another death
and defeat.
            I am anxious to get off the train to think
about myself. The train stops, the doors open
and the knifer is caught as he begins to leave.
He is beaten and dragged out and the stabbed person
bleeding on the floor is placed on a stretcher
and carried away. The train moves past me
and out of the station.
            I wish I knew where I

was going gladly, as it says on my appointment card.
I wish I could say I was going there as I go
trembling. The train has left me behind
to find my way upstairs to an exit,
the card a piece of paper in my hand.

VI

A New Theme

I chose for the first five sections of this book poems written all during Ignatow's life. The order is not chronological in any sense. But around 1964 or so, during the writing of *Rescue the Dead*, a new theme appeared.

I don't understand the theme very well, but I have made this section out of poems that move toward it. I can't describe the theme very well either, only allude to its edges. Its mood is of swift, highly sustained desire. In Lorca the Eros impulse is felt by the reader as absolutely indestructible—when Amnon looks at his sister naked on the roof, it's clear the desire he feels will have its way, and break through all brush dams set in its path, whether by private conscience or collective rules. In David Ignatow's poem "A Dialogue," a man wants to leap from a building to express sorrow. He knows that people will try to block him and send him away. Wherever they send him, he says, "I will go and die there in sorrow."

It is as if after the reasoning power of the ego has struggled for many years, chewing over issues of right and wrong, and trying to relate unknown material coming in from the unconscious to ethics, it has at last won through to some victory. The ego is stronger, and doesn't allow distraction. The gulls don't have any instinct quite like that, because their instincts, though firm, are nest-building instincts; in man the instinct has some element of self-destruction in it, and so the gulls seeing an open boat "veer off, afraid, afraid of a human." The movement is downward for the human being . . . he moves on stairs down into the personal unconscious . . . the walker longs to go down farther, but he is not sure "that these stairs were built by human hands."

It's clear that the power of the unnoticed, dark side, which showed itself earlier in images of goat smell clinging to the skin, of sudden violence from outdoors suddenly breaking into the family room, and finishing everyone off, images of an ineradicable primitive darkness, imagined as outside the ego, has now, after long invitation, sacrifice and struggle, slipped inside, come over the threshold, sat down by the fireplace, started to work with the ego, so as to make its decisions final.

This is probably the preparation for death that the ancients talked of, a stage of adulthood that in the fortunate man or woman precedes death. Evidently in death the bird will be nothing but his nest-building instinct and his triumph dance; the man will be nothing but his educated shadow, or as Yeats preferred to call it, his highest moment of will.

For My Daughter

When I die choose a star
and name it after me
that you may know
I have not abandoned
or forgotten you.
You were such a star to me,
following you through birth
and childhood, my hand
in your hand.
                When I die
choose a star and name it
after me so that I may shine
down on you, until you join
me in darkness and silence
together.

The Room

There's a door to my name
shutting me in, with a seat
at a table behind the wall
where I suck of the lemon seed.
Farther in is the bed
I have made of the fallen hairs
of my love, naked, her head dry.
I speak of the making of charts
and prescriptions and matches
that light tunnels
under the sea.

A chair, a table, a leg of a chair—
I hold these with my eyes to keep from falling,
my thoughts holding to these shapes,
my breathing of them that make my body
mine through the working of my eyes.
All else is silence and falling.

In the dark
I hear wings beating
and move my arms around
and above
to touch.
My arms go up and down
and around
as I circle the room.

Secretly

My foot awes me,
the cushion of the sole
in profile shaped like a bird's head,
the toes long and narrow like a beak,
the arch to the foot
with the gentle incline
of a bird's body
and the heel thick and stubby
like a starling's tail.
In a slow motion it ascends
and descends in a half-circle,
tense, poised for flight.
The full weight of my body
today walking on it
supporting me in my weariness
it can perform its flight,
its shape delicate, light,
swift-seeming, tense and tireless
as I lie on a bed, my foot
secretly a bird.

The Derelict

I'm going to be dead a long time,
says an old man, adjusting his trousers
in the public toilet. They hang down
below his buttocks, with legs spread apart,
he is tucking in his long underwear.
"I'll be dead a long time."

Lying curled up on the ground
against the wall, he is
a grey-haired foetus
which has given up
and returned to its mother.
Round and round she whirls
in space.

A Dialogue

I now will throw myself down
from a great height
to express sorrow.
Step aside, please.
I said please step aside
and permit me access
to the building's edge.
How is this, restrained,
encircled by arms,
in front of me a crowd?
I cannot be detained in this manner.
Hear me, I speak with normal emotion.
Release me,
I would express sorrow in its pure form.
I am insane, you say
and will send me away—
and I will go
and die there
in sorrow.

The Open Boat

With no place to lay my head
beside a friend
who could give peace,
none to guard my door
nor still my house,
I am five miles out: the sea
flexes its muscles
and I have gulls for companions
overhead—veering off,
afraid, afraid
of a human.

On the Death of Winston Churchill

Now should great men die
in turn one by one
to keep the mind solemn
and ordained,
the living attend in dark clothes
and with tender weariness
and crowds at television sets
and newsstands wait
as each man's death sustains a peace.
The great gone, the people
one by one
offer to die.

While I Live

I dream of language as the sun.
I whisper to that plant
whose own language is the wind.
It cups its flower to listen
at the wind's pressure and we talk
together of the darkness in language:
what Dante suffered at its command—
only that I may endure the necessary
ecstasy of my personal death.

I want my trees to love me
and my grass to reach up to the porch
where I am no one but the end of time,
as I stand waiting for renewal in my brain,
because I am what the sun shines forth:
I am labor, I am a disposition to live.
Who dies? Only the sun
but you must wait
while I live.

All Quiet

For Robert Bly
Written at the start of one of our bombing
pauses over North Vietnam

How come nobody is being bombed today?
I want to know, being a citizen
of this country and a family man.
You can't take my fate in your hands,
without informing me.
I can blow up a bomb or crush a skull—
whoever started this peace
without advising me
through a news leak
at which I could have voiced a protest,
running my whole family off a cliff.

An American Parable

Good boys are we to have retrieved
                                for its owner the ball
which first we dipped in liquid gold
                                with affection.
Now he keeps pitching it farther and farther,
curious, excited and alarmed,
nor can we understand,
since it is returned to him
each time heavier with gold
and less wieldly.

The Life Dance

I see bubbling out of the ground:
water, fresh, a pure smell. My mind
too begins to spring. I take
small hops. I enjoy myself
partly because I have the nerve.
Is anybody watching?
I care and don't care,
as I hop, and soon
because nobody is looking I'm leaping
and twisting into awkward shapes,
letting my hands make signs
of a meaning I do not understand.
I am absorbed in getting at what
till now
I had not been aware of.

There is a feeling in the world
I sometimes think I'm grasping.
I find myself holding a hand or
as I take a deep breath
I think it is there.

I wish I understood the beauty
in leaves falling. To whom
are we beautiful
as we go?

From a Dream

I'm on a stair going down.
I must get to a landing
where I can order food
and relax with a newspaper.
I should retrace my steps to be sure,
but the stairs above disappear into clouds.
But down is where I want to go,
these stairs were built to lead somewhere
and I would find out.
As I keep walking,
ever more slowly,
I leave notes such as this on the steps.
There must be an end to them
and I will get to it,
just as did the builders,
if only I were sure now
that these stairs were built
by human hands.

An Allegory

I offer my back to the silken net
to keep it from falling to the ground—
the smooth part of me,
silk would catch on my nails
the skein spread as far as I can see
across humped backs like mine.
Those straightening up
through a rip and looking about
say, "How everything shines."

Rescue the Dead

Finally, to forgo love is to kiss a leaf,
is to let rain fall nakedly upon your head,
is to respect fire,
is to study man's eyes and his gestures
as he talks,
is to set bread upon the table
and a knife discreetly by,
is to pass through crowds
like a crowd of oneself.
Not to love is to live.

To love is to be led away
into a forest where the secret grave
is dug, singing, praising darkness
under the trees.

To live is to sign your name,
is to ignore the dead,
is to carry a wallet
and shake hands.

To love is to be a fish.
My boat wallows in the sea.
You who are free,
rescue the dead.

An Afterword

Robert Lowell has expressed well the idea that our emotions are becoming less precise as mass civilization comes on, political life becomes hazy: "a savage servility slides by on grease." Certainly that is right. But what is becoming of us then? Lowell is not sure about that. One of Ignatow's ideas is that we are slowly slipping back toward the instincts. If European civilization could be described as a wooden floor, then we are sinking through wooden floors down to a stone floor, where the instincts make a pattern like those made by the dancers in Greek tragedies. When we arrive at the instinct level, a hundred years from now, people looking around will not find plastic emotions, mass indecisiveness, soggy feelings—as we would expect by projecting contemporary moods into the future—but rather clear and hard dances, grand and chilling. The living will join the dances, and be nourished again by their fathers.

David Ignatow's poems have an unusual openness to the consciousness of the collective. We are more used to poets open to the personal unconscious. If the "dark side" is thought of as a part of the personal unconscious, we notice that David Ignatow sees his dark side clearly only after he has seen it reflected in the angers and frustrations of the collective, when he sees it embodied in a stabber moving through a subway car. He is a poet of the community, of people who work for a living, as Whitman was too, but he is also a great poet of the collective. Reading him we experience in a deep way our union with the collective. An example is David Ignatow's poem on the death of Winston Churchill, whose death was a part of the collective consciousness.

> The great gone, the people
> one by one
> offer to die.

David Ignatow says that we are so caught up in it that we pass through a crowd "like a crowd of oneself." As he declares in "Rescue the Dead," to live that way is not to love. He recognizes that nine-tenths of our "love" is ordered love,

love we undertake at the demand of the civilization, idealistic love, humanistic love. Nothing comes of it. All that, whether we wish it or no, is ending.

"Rescue the Dead" is a mysterious and marvellous poem, in which the meanings of "to live" and "to be dead" keep shifting, as well as the meanings of "to love" and "to be alive." There is some sort of ecstasy in the poem as well, perhaps from having faced these intricate ideas so imaginatively.

Like Rilke, Ignatow notices that human emotions are not becoming less insistent, but more insistent, and they have greater influence upon events. The sorrow cannot be dissipated. The stairs he goes down in a dream, if not "built by human hands," then perhaps were built by God, or by hard, chill instincts. The poem with those stairs in it is another hint that Western man is moving again into the nonhuman, into a state that interested the Greeks.

It is thought that rituals are a form that instinct behavior takes in human beings, modified by civilization. It is interesting that Ignatow has written three "Rituals."

His work says that we are caught in the collective consciousness, and therefore we are unable to rescue the dead, who now live helpless in that vast consciousness, longing to be rescued. "You who are free, rescue the dead." I think one of David Ignatow's loveliest qualities is that unlike Shelley, who claims he is free and we are all imprisoned, Ignatow does not claim to be free. He asks those who are free to rescue the dead.